WANICK FAYETTE

JOEL

I0461741

Finding the Blessing in
The Lesson Of Destruction

*TO AMARA, MY BEAUTIFUL WIFE, THANKYOU FOR ALL OF YOUR SUPPORT,
I LOVE YOU.*

ABOUT THE AUTHOR

Born in Haiti and brought to America at the age of three, Wanick Fayette grew up in an impoverished community with his older brothers, who fascinated him with their connection to the Spiritual side of their faith in practice. These experiences set his heart on fire for it, and at the age of five, he began to understand the impact faith and spiritual practices would have on his life.

At an early age, Pastor Wanick became involved with the Acts 2 Ministry, sponsored by the local Baptist church. Through this program, he came to know the LORD. At the urban youth camp, Kid's Across America, KAA YOU KNOW!!, he surrendered his life to the LORD. The search for freedom from sinful bondage led Pastor Wanick to grow in the WORD. Pastor Wanick attended Liberty University and earned His Bachelor of Science Degree as a Certified Health Educational Specialist. After receiving his degree, Pastor Wanick's goal was to attend medical school and become a doctor. God had other plans. After much prayer and fasting, Pastor Wanick heard God's calling for him to enter Full-time Ministry. Pastor Wanick married his beautiful wife Amara, a stunning woman, on December 18, 2016. Pastor Wanick, Amara, and their dog, Basil, moved to Johnstown, Pennsylvania in 2016 where he and his wife became foster parents. In 2018, Wanick became pastor of Beulah Church. As a spiritual leader, Pastor Wanick exhibits his favorite Bible passage through his actions and words, Luke 9:23: "Then he said to them all, "If anyone desires to come after Me, let him deny himself, and take up his cross daily, and follow Me." Pastor Wanick earned his Master of Divinity from United Theological Seminary and is now Pastor of two churches in the Greater Johnstown area.

For more info go to www.WanickFayette.com

Introduction

I was never really one to write introductions, but being this book has had such an impact over my life, I would feel foolish If I did not write one. I started writing Joel Finding the blessing in the Lesson of Destruction in the middle of the pandemic. As I was doing the research and studying for what I believe God has called me to do, everything in my life was going great.

I was in seminary, and everything was going great with the church I was pastoring, and I was walking on sunshine. I started to think to myself, "man this will be a great book/devotional for someone going through a hard time." As I am writing this now, I can hear God say, "you have no idea." As the year went on, me and my family had a few Covid scares but nothing too serious until I got Covid.

What started as the flu in a matter of days turned into full-on COVID-19. I could not move. I could barely breathe. I remember it like it was yesterday. I told my wife I was going to bed to sleep it off. I did not want to go to the hospital. As I was trying to sleep, the coughing would not stop, and the sweats were soaking my whole bed. My wife came upstairs to the room because of my coughing (I am glad she did). She told me I needed to go to the E.R because I did not look good. I told her, no I am ok. She would not take no for an answer. Praise God she did not. We get to the E.R and as I am in the hospital room on a ventilator holding on for dear life; the doctor walks in and says, "so how long have you had diabetes?"

Wow, God, diabetes!! Me, the person who works out five times a week. Me, the person who fasts for weeks on end. Me, the person who does everything "right." I lay there in shock and do not know what to say. Well, I knew what to say. I told the Doctor I do not have diabetes. He said," yes you do and according to your numbers you have had it for some time now. If your wife did not bring you in, you would have slipped into a diabetic coma." It was after hearing those words did my heart drop.

I was kept in the hospital for over a week and a half and in my room where I was alone, all I knew to do was talk to God. This is when the book came back to my mind. When I said this book would be great for someone going through a tough time, it would be me that would need it. My world was flipped upside down, much like the people of Israel in the book of Joel. In their destruction, God provided a lesson that came as a blessing.

As you go through this book, I pray that if you are going through something, it may be shocking news, pain, hurt, or spiritual drought. I pray you standfast and continue to trust in the LORD. If you are reading this book and you simply want to grow more in your understanding of the book of Joel, then God bless you and I pray that he keeps you.

This book was a lifeline for me and my family and some others who had the opportunity to read it before publication. May the fruits of this book be a beacon to your spiritual walk and may it strengthen your trust in the LORD.

So back to my story. I get better, Goodbye Covid. But I was still diagnosed with diabetes. I have learned to press into the LORD, even more, when life happens, and he will guide and lead you into His presence. Currently, my numbers are normal. I went from a 15 A1C to a 5.6 A1C, Praise God! I am not making any health guarantees as you read and study this book. What I am saying is it will change your life because you read and studied this book. May God be with you in all that you do. God bless.

Now, how are you supposed to read this book? The answer is quite simple. There are 6 days of devotional studies every week. This will fill 6 days of your week. On the seventh day, you should be in church to get fed spiritually. Then you start the next week and repeat the cycle. This book will effectively fill one hundred days of your year as it is 17 weeks long. There are challenges each day after every devotional. I encourage you to try them. You will find that the LORD is closer than you have ever thought.

Happy Reading, God bless. Wanick Fayette

Joel
Finding the Blessing in
the Lesson of Destruction

1 The word of the Lord that came to Joel son of Pethuel:

2 Hear this, you elders;

listen, all you inhabitants of the land.

Has anything like this ever happened in your days

or in the days of your ancestors?

3 Tell your children about it,

and let your children tell their children,

and their children the next generation.

4 What the devouring locust has left,

the swarming locust has eaten;

what the swarming locust has left,

the young locust has eaten;

and what the young locust has left,

the destroying locust has eaten.

Week One-Day 1

VERSE 2
Hear this, you elders;

listen, all you inhabitants of the land.

Has anything like this ever happened in your days

or in the days of your ancestors?

We start out in the book of Joel with Joel giving a warning to the people of Israel. He first starts out with the Elders of Israel then he addresses all the inhabitants of the Land. Why call the elders first? The elders were the leaders of the communities of the different houses in Israel. If there was ever any issue, you would first go to the elders before you go to anyone else. He then questions them, and asks them, has anything like this happened before? The answer is a solid yes, but not to us, it happened to the people of Egypt, but this time it is happening to the people of Israel.

God is trying to get the attention of His people. He begins with the individuals who are in leadership. Leaders, Parents, Teachers, this is for you. When God wants to relay a message to the church, family, or student you are over, he is going to come through you. You are the one who must be willing and always ready to hear from God first before those under you.

CHALLENGE
Today, I want you to think about your attitude towards listening to God. How has God been calling you to lead? Are you listening? If not, what can you do to listen better? Are you in a place of leadership that you should be ever ready to receive instruction from God? If you are in such a place, are you ready to listen and obey?

YOUR REFLECTIONS:

VERSE 3

Tell your children about it,

and let your children tell their children,

and their children the next generation.

We see here that after the elders are told of this disaster then the people are told. After the people are told, they are then told to tell their children. And the children are told to tell their children and so on and so forth. What is happening in Israel is so bad that the people do not ever want to forget about what happened to them at that specific time in history.

Go and tell your children what is happening right now. And tell them to tell their children. Tell them about the work that God is doing in your life. Tell them about How you found a blessing in the midst of destruction. Pass down all the great things of God both good and bad. Because it is God who allows the Locust to come, and it is God who takes the locust away

CHALLENGE

What is God doing in your life right now, that he is calling you to share with those around you? Do you only share the good parts of your faith? If so, why? I challenge you to share the tough parts of your faith. You never know, you might just see the blessing in the ashes.

YOUR REfLECTIONS:

VERSE 4

What the <u>devouring locust</u> has left,

the swarming locust has eaten;

what the swarming locust has left,

the young locust has eaten;

and what the young locust has left,

the destroying locust has eaten.

We now are looking at the destruction that is upon the People of Israel. The destruction came in the way of locust. Locust are like grasshoppers, but when they come you better head for the hills. They destroy everything in their path. In the first part of verse four, we read of the devouring locust. The devouring locust here represent the destruction that came upon the Israelites quickly. It came upon the people, and they were not prepared.

The devouring locust can show up in our lives in many ways. By way of a terrifying phone call or by way of a sudden change in lifestyle, whatever it may be, we are never truly prepared for when it comes. And since we are not prepared, the way of handling the situation is a little too late.

CHALLENGE

How have the devouring locust shown up in your life lately? Were you prepared? What was the lesson that you feel God was trying to teach you? Or was he giving you a warning? Today, I want you to sit and examine your life to find those devouring locusts, and see why God allowed them to be a part of your life.

YOUR REFLECTIONS:

VERSE 4

What the devouring locust has left,

the swarming locust has eaten;

what the swarming locust has left,

the young locust has eaten;

and what the young locust has left,

the destroying locust has eaten.

What the devouring locust have left, the swarming locust have eaten. Why four kinds of locust? Destruction comes in our lives in many ways. Destruction can come quickly (devouring locust) and destruction can move into our lives and form residency (swarming locust). This is the type of destruction that you just cannot seem to shake. If it is not one thing, it is another. This destruction can be compared to going through the storms of life. The good thing about going through a storm is that it does not last forever. Just like a storm, the swarming locust never last forever as we see in the second part of the verse.

The swarming locust are the problems that you just cannot seem to shake. You get through the swarm the same way you get through the storm by prayer and steadfastness in the LORD.

CHALLENGE

Destruction will come into your life and stay for a while. How do you plan to get through the swarm? Today, I want you to sit and examine your life to find those swarming locusts. You will not have to look hard; they have been there for a while. Look to see why God has allowed them to be a part of your life.

YOUR Reflections:

VERSE 4

What the devouring locust has left,

the swarming locust has eaten;

what the swarming locust has left,

the young locust has eaten;

and what the young locust has left,

the destroying locust has eaten.

Whatever remains after the swarming locust leave, the young locusts eat. What are the young locusts? The young locust represents the destruction that comes upon the immature and the inexperienced, those who are still wet behind the ears. This plague that God sent to the people of Israel is the result of the people turning away against God. This is not the first time that this has happen. Simply look at Israel's past. We know that the only type of people who make the same mistakes more than once are the young and inexperienced.

This type of destruction appears in your life when you are making the same mistakes repeatedly. The destruction in your life that is happening because of pure immaturity means you must grow up. Growing up is not just for adulthood, but it is for your faith too. You must go from milk to meat. The healing comes in the maturity of the person. You will find just as in adulthood, the mistakes made as a youth are not the same as ones made by an adult.

CHALLENGE

The young locust come into our lives simply for the sake of our immaturity. There are problems you may be facing right now simply because you just will not grow up. Today, look for those young locusts that are causing destruction in your life. Today, I want you to sit and examine your life to find those young locusts. Look to see why God has allowed them to be a part of your life.

YOUR REFLECTIONS:

VERSE 4

What the devouring locust has left,

the swarming locust has eaten;

what the swarming locust has left,

the young locust has eaten;

and what the young locust has left,

the destroying locust has eaten.

We are now at the destroying locust. What the young locust have left, the destroying locust have eaten. The destroying locust represent the complete destruction of the land. First destruction came quickly (devouring locust). Then it made residence and stayed in the land (swarming locust). The problem of repeating the same mistakes (young locust) caused it to keep returning and thus destroyed the land completely.

This is how destruction comes into our lives. It comes swiftly when we are not prepared. Because we are not prepared, it stays longer and swarms our lives. It is sometimes because of our immaturity in the faith that these things keep happening to us. When you add all of these, destruction comes and destroys our lives. As a believer in Jesus Christ, do understand that destruction is coming. However, do understand that we serve the God that can send the destruction and remove the destruction.

CHALLENGE

Understanding how destruction comes into our lives is vital. How can you prepare to better handle the adversity that comes with your spiritual faith? Has there been destroying locust in your life? If so where? I invite you to pray this prayer with me.

God, thank you for all that you have done for me. I thank you for the devouring locust. I thank you for the swarming locust. I thank you for the young locust, and I thank you for the destroying locust. Lord, thank you for calling me to do better and to grow more in my faith. Open my eyes that I may find the blessing in the lesson of destruction. AMEN

YOUR REFLECTIONS:

5 Wake up, you drunkards, and weep;

wail, all you wine drinkers,

because of the sweet wine,

for it has been taken from your mouth.

6 For a nation has invaded my land,

powerful and without number;

its teeth are the teeth of a lion,

and it has the fangs of a lioness.

7 It has devastated my grapevine

and splintered my fig tree.

It has stripped off its bark and thrown it away;

its branches have turned white.

8 Grieve like a young woman dressed in sackcloth,

mourning for the husband of her youth.

9 Grain and drink offerings have been cut off

from the house of the Lord;

the priests, who are ministers of the Lord, mourn.

10 The fields are destroyed;

the land grieves;

indeed, the grain is destroyed;

the new wine is dried up;

and the fresh oil fails.

11 Be ashamed, you farmers,

wail, you vinedressers,[a]

over the wheat and the barley,

because the harvest of the field has perished.

12 The grapevine is dried up,

and the fig tree is withered;

the pomegranate, the date palm, and the apple—

all the trees of the orchard—have withered.

Indeed, human joy has dried up.

VERSE 5

5 Wake up, you drunkards, and weep;

wail, all you wine drinkers,

because of the sweet wine,

for it has been taken from your mouth.

As the Locusts are invading the Land, we hear a call for the drunkards and wine drinkers to get up. Why call for the drinkers to get up in the time of crisis? This was God calling to get the attention of His people. He first calls the drinkers to get their attention. Those who drink to get drunk use this as a sort of grieving and coping mechanism. God calls them to look and see that the plants for their wine are being destroyed by the destruction that is happening around them. He wants their eyes to be open to what he is doing so that their running is not to the bottle (because there isn't any) but to run to Him.

Your wine is running out and your cup is running dry. God wants you to pay attention. He sends disasters to get your attention away from your many coping mechanisms. It is taken from your mouth and you thirst. To whom will you run to quench your thirst?

CHALLENGE
God wants to get your attention today. He calls the people by what the coping mechanism they use. To those who drink, he called them Drunkards. To those who drink wine, He called them wine drinkers. What would He call you? Are you ready to give up your coping mechanism for something greater?

YOUR REflECTIONS:

VERSE 6-7

6 For a nation has invaded my land, powerful and without number; its teeth are the teeth of a lion, and it has the fangs of a lioness.

7 It has devastated my grapevine and splintered my fig tree. It has stripped off its bark and thrown it away; its branches have turned white.

Why should the people wake up? The invaders are in the land, and they are destroying the nation. Attention is called to the invaders. God calls His people to look at and to take notice of the invaders. Look at the destruction that is happening. The numbers are great. They are fierce, and they devastate all that is in their path.

As destruction happens around us and to us, we are called to take notice. God calls us to pay attention to what is going on around us. Take note of the sadness. Take notice of the horror and pain. See what God is allowing in your life and wait. Lift your eyes to the hills, and see where your help comes from. Take notice of the destruction, because when the healing and the rebuilding happens, it will make the view that much more beautiful.

CHALLENGE

Are your eyes open? Are you paying attention to the destruction that is happening around you? Today, take notice of your surroundings. Take it all in. The healing will be that much more beautiful!

YOUR REFLECTIONS:

VERSE 8

8 Grieve like a young woman dressed in sackcloth,

mourning for the husband of her youth.

The people wake up. They see the destruction, and they are called to mourn. Cry, don't hold it in, let it all out. This is not, I had a bad day type of crying. But I just lost the love of my life who was my best friend, and I know I will never see them again on this side of eternity. This is the type of mourning that is to be done as destruction is happening.

When life hits us, our basic instinct is to hold it in and keep moving forward. That sounds good, but sometimes, you just need to let it out. We are not to hold in the pain and sorrow. We are to grieve and cry out to the LORD, because He is the friend that sticks closer than a brother.

CHALLENGE

Is your heart heavy right now? Ask yourself, what are you holding on to that the LORD wants you to let go of. Once you find what it is, LET IT GO! Grieving is not simply about crying it out, but learning to let go of what hurts us, and keeps us bound from finding freedom in who God is.

YOUR REFLECTIONS:

VERSE 9-10

9 Grain and drink offerings have been cut off

from the house of the Lord;

the priests, who are ministers of the Lord, mourn.

10 The fields are destroyed;

the land grieves;

indeed, the grain is destroyed;

the new wine is dried up;

and the fresh oil fails.

Offerings to the LORD are now cut off. The priests of God are now mourning. The land is grieving, and everything is dried up. God allows destruction to come upon his own people so bad that drink offerings are cut off from the LORD. God is more concerned about his people turning towards Him. He would rather have the offerings that are due Him cut off then allow the people to continue to rebel against Him and His law.

God is more concerned about your obedience towards him than he is about your sacrifice towards Him. If you are not obedient to God's Word, then it doesn't matter what you do in your good conscience, it will never matter to God.

CHALLENGE

God desires obedience over sacrifice. Check your heart today. Is your sacrifice more than your obedience to God? Or is it the other way around?

YOUR REfLECTIONS:

VERSE 11

11 Be ashamed, you farmers,

wail, you vinedressers,

over the wheat and the barley,

because the harvest of the field has perished.

The attention of the farmers and vinedressers are now called. They are to be put to shame. Why so cruel, you may ask? The farmers who grew the grain were the ones responsible for not only growing the grain, but also keeping enough in storage if ever a famine was to happen. Famine happened, and where were the farmers overflow? Where was the extra that was put into storage? There was none. This is why they should be put to shame. They failed to prepare in a position that calls them to prep for famine (hard times).

We are called to pay attention and watch the times. Disaster comes upon us swiftly, and we seldom have time to prepare. We must learn to prepare for famine in this life. Famine is common, it can manifest in many different ways. Be on your guard, and be sober minded ready to welcome the blade of destruction.

CHALLENGE

Destruction is coming, are you ready? Have you planned adequately for such a time as this? Today plan your heart and mind for the famines of life. PRAY, FAST, ASK God for strength, and rest in who He is. This will prepare you for destruction.

YOUR REFLECTIONS:

VERSE 12

12 The grapevine is dried up,

and the fig tree is withered;

the pomegranate, the date palm, and the apple—

all the trees of the orchard—have withered.

Indeed, human joy has dried up.

Amidst the famine, there is also a drought in the land. All these fruit names are common for flowing with flavor. Even the Joy of Man is dried up. Where there is no Joy, there is no Hope. The people's attention was called to see all that the LORD allowed to happen to His people for one purpose, to turn to Him and be prepared for the destruction.

Life can suck the joy right out of our hearts. What was once flowing is now withered and dry. There's no life. Recognize where you are when destruction is against you. Where is your Hope?

CHALLENGE

We are called to be vigilant. We are to have our eyes open. Our hope is in the LORD. Yes, He allows the destruction to happen in our lives, but He gives us every opportunity to turn to Him and seek refuge. Today run to Him for His name is a strong tower.

Pray with me: LORD you are good, and you are God. I thank you for the famine and destruction that you allow into my life to draw me closer to you. GOD, I want you more. Continue to draw me to you. LORD let me see your hand over my life. LORD let me Find the Blessing in the Lesson of Destruction. Be my comfort. In Jesus name I pray amen.

YOUR REflECTIONS:

13 Dress in sackcloth and lament,
you priests;

wail, you ministers of the altar.

Come and spend the night in
sackcloth,

you ministers of my God,

because grain and drink offerings

are withheld from the house of your
God.

14 Announce a sacred fast;

proclaim a solemn assembly!

Gather the elders

and all the residents of the land

at the house of the Lord your God,

and cry out to the Lord.

VERSE 13

13 <u>Dress in sackcloth and lament, you priests;</u>

wail, you ministers of the altar.

Come and spend the night in sackcloth,

you ministers of my God,

because grain and drink offerings

are withheld from the house of your God.

While in destruction, the priests are left with nothing to do. There are no grain and fruit offerings. There's famine in the land, and the livestock is suffering. All animals are affected. How can they bring God the best of their livestock when all animals are affected by the famine? There are none that is perfect worthy of sacrifice. In times like this, the only thing to do is to lament. Expressing all the grief and sorrow that you are feeling.

The priest had one job which was to make offerings to the LORD. That job was taken from them. When life hits you and takes all that you have, sometimes the best thing to do is to let it out. Shout, weep, cry, and most importantly, seek the LORD. When destruction comes, you may lose the very thing you were dependent on.

CHALLENGE

Today, look at your profession in your destruction. Do you still have your job? Your source of income is it still providing for your family? If so, praise God, you are blessed. If not, have you lamented to the LORD yet, or are you holding it in? It is ok to let it out. There is nothing wrong with crying in the Father's hands.

YOUR REFLECTIONS:

VERSE 13
13 Dress in sackcloth and lament, you priests;

wail, you ministers of the altar.

Come and spend the night in sackcloth,

you ministers of my God,

because grain and drink offerings

are withheld from the house of your God.

Wail! Cry and scream child of God. Your job is gone, and you have nothing. You are in the same boat as everyone else. Go and be in reflection with the LORD your God. Take a day. This is what Joel is saying to the ministers of the altar. Often when one wears sackcloth, they are hurt, and recognize they have sinned against the Lord. They are in deep anguish. So, they put on sackcloth to let themselves, as well as others know, everything is not ok. Spend the night in sackcloth. It is ok to take a day, O man of God.

When destruction hits close to home, sometimes the best thing to do in the pain is to take a nap or sleep on it. It may seem cavalier but being able to find rest in pain and anguish, gives your body time to adjust to the circumstance that are in your life presently.

CHALLENGE
Everything is not OK, and that's ok. Destruction happens. Take a day to yourself and reflect. Seek God and sleep. Today, if you have not already done so, take a nap. Wail first then nap. The God that takes your burden will give you rest.

YOUR REFLECTIONS:

VERSE 13
13 Dress in sackcloth and lament, you priests;

wail, you ministers of the altar.

Come and spend the night in sackcloth,

you ministers of my God,

because grain and drink offerings

are withheld from the house of your God.

Why wail? Why lament? The priest offerings were affected by the destruction of the locust. Their work was affected. Their salary was affected by the destruction that was going on around them. What they would normally offer, they can't and that makes life hard. And the best thing they knew to do was to cry out to the LORD their God.

Your salary is affected. Your hours have changed. You do not know when or how you are going to make ends meet. You do not know what to bring to the LORD, because you feel like everything has been taken away from you. You are to lift your eyes up to the hills and see where your hope comes from. Destruction happens and those who belong to the LORD see God in the storm.

CHALLENGE
Time to face the music. Now what? Today, what are you going to do when your comfort is gone? I would encourage you to ask God to give you eyes to see the help that he has placed around you. It does not matter what you lack in your giving department. He will take your little. It is there that you will be encouraged.

YOUR REFLECTIONS:

VERSE 14

14 <u>Announce a sacred fast;</u>

proclaim a solemn assembly!

Gather the elders

and all the residents of the land

at the house of the Lord your God,

and cry out to the Lord.

There is nothing left to do. Wail, lament, sleep on it. Now it is time to fast. Announce a sacred fast. This fast is a full denial of one's self. No food, only water. This is a place where the people of God can meet God face to face.

Part of healing is going to God empty handed. Why go on a fast in the middle of not having anything? You must go to God with what you have and surrender it all. The great thing about a fast is that it shows you have more than you thought you ever did. Because when it is time to give it up onto the LORD, it is when you realize how much you neglected what you already had. In addition, you realize how much it hurts to give it up and away to the LORD.

CHALLENGE

God desires obedience over sacrifice. Check your heart today. Is your sacrifice more than your obedience to God? Or is it the other way around?

YOUR REFLECTIONS:

VERSE 14

14 Announce a sacred fast;

proclaim a solemn assembly!

Gather the elders

and all the residents of the land

at the house of the Lord your God,

and cry out to the Lord.

In the storm of destruction, the fast is not for the single person, but it is for the community. They called the elders and the residents of the land to the house of the LORD. Everyone was to come and participate in this fast. And the place that it was done was in the presence of the LORD. What better way to seek God than in His very presence?

In your storm, Invite others to a group fast. Go to a retreat or go out in nature to see God in all His creation. The whole world is His, so you can literally go anywhere secluded to meet God. The point is, not to do it alone. This fight is just as much spiritual as it is physical.

CHALLENGE

When was the last time you fasted unto the LORD? What did you give up and what was your goal? Today I want you to plan out a day of fasting. Ask a friend, someone who is willing to fight with you and to fast with you. You will find that the battle is that much more peaceful when you have a battle buddy.

YOUR REflECTIONS:

VERSE 14

14 Announce a sacred fast;

proclaim a solemn assembly!

Gather the elders

and all the residents of the land

at the house of the Lord your God,

and cry out to the Lord.

What does it mean to cry? Why repeat it so many times? It is through crying that our inner most emotions come out unfiltered. Whether it is a heartfelt cry or a happy cry, or a sad cry, those tears that come out are full of emotions and feelings that just would not be expressed with words alone. The LORD hears the tears of His people

Your pain is not unnoticed. Let it out. As scripture says, God will wipe away every tear from our eyes when we see him. The scripture also tells us that he hears our tears, and He is always listening for the real and honest us. When that person shows up, we are there naked before a holy and loving God that is ready and willing to LOVE us in all our brokenness so cry out to God. He is listening.

CHALLENGE
Today, I call you to be ready to be open and intimate with God like never before. He is waiting to see and hear all your hurts and emotions.

Pray with me: LORD you are good, and you are God. I thank you for the ability to cry out to you as Father. God I cannot do this alone. I need you and I lay here open, holding back nothing from your love. Heal me lord and continue to draw me to you. AMEN

YOUR REFLECTIONS:

15 Woe because of that day!

For the day of the Lord is near

and will come as devastation from the Almighty.

16 Hasn't the food been cut off

before our eyes,

joy and gladness

from the house of our God?

17 The seeds lie shriveled in their casings.

The storehouses are in ruin,

and the granaries are broken down,

because the grain has withered away.

18 How the animals groan!

The herds of cattle wander in confusion

since they have no pasture.

Even the flocks of sheep and goats suffer punishment.

19 I call to you, Lord,

for fire has consumed

the pastures of the wilderness,

and flames have devoured

all the trees of the orchard.

20 Even the wild animals cry out to you,

for the river beds are dried up,

and fire has consumed

the pastures of the wilderness.

VERSE 15

15 Woe because of that day!

For the day of the Lord is near

and will come as devastation from the Almighty.

Woe because of that day! Woe, what does woe mean? Woe means great sorrow or distress. Joel is speaking to the people of Israel and tells them that great sorrow and distress is heading their way. Understanding that impending doom is on the horizon is one thing, to have it come from God is another statement. The LORD is bringing the day of the LORD himself.

The day of the LORD is coming. God is bringing it to your front door. How do you plan on facing such destruction? There is HOPE in the day of the LORD. It is the LORD's, and this is our HOPE. We need not fear what the LORD brings, because he makes all things work for the good of those who trust Him.

CHALLENGE

The LORD works all things for the good of those who love God, to those who are the called according to His purpose. Do you, and can you, find comfort in such a statement? Do you love God? Today check your heart and see where you are in this verse. I encourage you to read Romans 6:23 and Romans 10:9-10.

YOUR REFLECTIONS:

VERSE 16
16 Hasn't the food been cut off

before our eyes,

joy and gladness

from the house of our God?

Signs of the day of the LORD are here. Have you not noticed the lack of food? Where is your joy? It is gone, and there is nothing left. Your very place of worship does not carry the same energy that it once carried. It has become a chore to go into the house of the LORD, because so much destruction has surrounded you that the idea of going to church seams pointless.

Often when destruction happens in our lives, the very first place we should go to is the very place that we are running away from. We say, "I have so many things going on right now, I'll come to church when I get my life right." Such a statement says to us that we do not feel worthy to be in the presence of God right now. He doesn't want the broken me, he wants the fixed me. Nothing can be further from the truth. Your joy maybe gone, but God is still in the house of God. He doesn't change places based on your circumstances. You can find Him where he has always been, right in the church.

CHALLENGE
Today, go to the place where you feel like you are not worthy to be at and pray. It is there that God wants to meet and heal you. You are meant to be there.

YOUR REFLECTIONS:

VERSE 17
17 The seeds lie shriveled in their casings.

The storehouses are in ruin,

and the granaries are broken down,

because the grain has withered away.

There is no food. The storehouses for the grain are broken down because there is no grain. Nothing is left. What is there to store if there is no food? Why go to the harvest when there is nothing to harvest? Why store for the future when there may be no future? There is nothing.

The seeds are dying, the granaries are not in use, because there is no grain for threshing. Why go through the trouble of putting in the hours when there is no pay to receive? These are the effects of the day of the LORD. Everything is made pointless or without reason. No matter how hard we may try, all things are in the LORD's hands, and we must rest in His arms

CHALLENGE
Have you been fighting the LORD in your destruction? Are you trying to keep things afloat when everything else is drowning? Today, I challenge you to let it go. If it is lost in the destruction, let it be. Don't try to hold onto everything and lose sight of the LORD.

YOUR REFLECTIONS:

VERSE 18
18 How the animals groan!

The herds of cattle wander in confusion

since they have no pasture.

Even the flocks of sheep and goats suffer punishment.

It is not just the people of God that are affected by such a disaster, but it is also the animals. The punishment of the people of Israel goes far beyond just the people but also everything that is connected to said people. The granaries, the plants, the food, and the livestock. When the LORD judges, it does not simply affect the person but the community.

The destruction is not just affecting you, but your surroundings, your community, those who are under you in a place of leadership, and your family. With such an understanding, the plan should be to lead all closer to the LORD in this time of destruction.

CHALLENGE
Today, look at those around you. When destruction comes, they will be affected in some way, shape or form. How do you plan on leading them? I encourage you to pray and seek guidance.

YOUR REFLECTIONS:

VERSE 19
19 I call to you, Lord,

for fire has consumed

the pastures of the wilderness,

and flames have devoured

all the trees of the orchard.

A cry goes out to the LORD to plead for the fire that is destroying the land. Destruction is happening everywhere and now the man of God is crying out to the LORD. He is officially lamenting, and the LORD hears him.

In your destruction, how long did it take you to cry out to the LORD? This usually takes some time. We are often in too deep before we recognize that we need help.

CHALLENGE
Today, if destruction is at your door, cry out now. Now is the time to seek the Lord.

YOUR REFLECTIONS:

VERSE 20

20 Even the wild animals cry out to you,

for the river beds are dried up,

and fire has consumed

the pastures of the wilderness.

The animals cry out because the rivers are dry. There is a drought in the land, and they are suffering. The water is the life sustaining factor that is needed. Destruction by fire and drought, what more is left? How much more can that punishment last and can the people of God take?

This is your surroundings crying out to the LORD. Sometimes this is in response to your faithfulness or it is because of your lack of faith. Nevertheless, the crying out will happen. You are charged to lead that cry of need for the LORD.

CHALLENGE

Today, cry out to the LORD. He is listening. Do you know what to say? Look around and find what is on your heart to pray.

Pray with me: LORD you are good, and you are God. I surrender to your LOVE. I surrender to your power. I CANNOT DO THIS. I need you. Amen

YOUR Reflections:

1 Blow the ram's horn in Zion;

sound the alarm on my holy
mountain!

Let all the residents of the land
tremble,

for the day of the Lord is coming;

in fact, it is near—

2 a day of darkness and gloom,

a day of clouds and total darkness,

like the dawn spreading over the
mountains;

a great and strong people appears,

such as never existed in ages past

and never will again

in all the generations to come.

Week Five-Day 1

VERSE 1
1 <u>Blow the ram's horn in Zion;</u>

<u>sound the alarm on my holy mountain!</u>

Let all the residents of the land tremble,

for the day of the Lord is coming;

in fact, it is near—

Alert, alert! Sound the alarm! Something was headed in the direction of Israel that they were not ready for. Sound the alarm! Where should they sound the alarm? The place they are called to sound the alarm is the mountain of God. Why the mountain of God? This is where revelation happens, where God redeems His people and leads them.

When you are on high alert where do you go to sound the alarm? What is the point of sounding the alarm when the danger is already there? The point is to alert those who are asleep. To wake those up who have not been watching for the coming doom. You are to alert the people of coming doom in the place where God redeems and heals His people, and that is His holy mountain.

CHALLENGE
Where is <u>your</u> holy mountain? The place where you retreat when you alert others of the coming doom? Is it your prayer closet or is it your church? Today I want you to establish a mountain where you go to meet God for any reason, especially impending doom.

YOUR REFLECTIONS:

Week Five-Day 2

VERSE 1

1 Blow the ram's horn in Zion;

sound the alarm on my holy mountain!

<u>Let all the residents of the land tremble,</u>

<u>for the day of the Lord is coming;</u>

in fact, it is near—

Let everyone tremble before the coming day of the LORD. The Day of the LORD is coming. What should the attitude of the people be but to shake involuntarily, typically because of anxiety, excitement, or frailty. The people are called to tremble before the coming day of the LORD.

The day of the LORD is coming. What should be your attitude? You can either shake involuntarily because of anxiety, excitement, or frailty. Which is the one that you will choose? Those who have no regard for the LORD will be shaking from anxiety or frailty. However, the one who waits on the LORD will be shaking with excitement.

CHALLENGE

How will you be trembling when the Day of the LORD comes? Today examine your heart and you will find your answer.

YOUR REfLECTIONS:

31

VERSE 1

1 Blow the ram's horn in Zion;

sound the alarm on my holy mountain!

Let all the residents of the land tremble,

for the day of the Lord is coming;

<u>in fact, it is near</u>—

The time you think you have belongs to God. There is no time to plan or act. The People of Israel had no time to prepare, therefore, they had to alert everyone of the coming day of the LORD.

We often think that we have extra time. The truth in the matter is our time is running out. When we play with time, we often find that we lose time. This is in direct result of our mismanagement of a precious gift of God. You will not always have time when you get older to make the decision. The time is now. The day of the LORD is near.

CHALLENGE

You do not have time to make the decision when you are older or until you get your life together. The fact is, the day of the LORD is near. Are you ready?

YOUR REFLECTIONS:

VERSE 2

2 <u>a day of darkness and gloom,</u>	such as never existed in ages past
<u>a day of clouds and total darkness,</u>	and never will again
like the dawn spreading over the mountains;	in all the generations to come.
a great and strong people appears,	

It is amazing that when the day of the LORD comes, it will be a day of darkness. The light of the sun will not be seen.   This is total darkness over the whole land of Israel.

With the lack of sunlight, in total darkness, there is a lack of Hope. Why a lack of Hope? The lack of Hope comes from the time running out. The lack of Hope comes from not be able to escape the coming of God's wrath on creation. Thus, total darkness is the perfect picture for the lack of Hope.

CHALLENGE
No hope, no peace. Know God, know peace. There will be a lack of Hope for those who do not trust God. For those who trust God, there is Hope in the name of Jesus Christ. Today if you are not sure, pray that your eyes would be open to who He is.

YOUR REflECTIONS:

VERSE 2

2 a day of darkness and gloom,	such as never existed in ages past
a day of clouds and total darkness,	and never will again
like the dawn spreading over the mountains;	in all the generations to come.
a great and strong people appears,	

This army that is coming upon the land is big and vast. This army is so big that Joel describes it as nightfall covering the mountain. What is man to do in the face of the army that belongs to the LORD? THE ANSWER: NOTHING.

When the LORD comes, he will come with an army that is unstoppable. They will come with strength and power, and there is nothing that you or I can do about it. Destruction is coming that we cannot stop. When you cannot beat them join them. By joining them, I mean to lean into it. When in Rome, do as the Romans do.

CHALLENGE
Today, lean into the destruction that is in your life right now. This is a type of destruction that cannot be avoided. Whatever it maybe in your life, Trust God and lean into it.

YOUR REFLECTIONS:

VERSE 2

2 a day of darkness and gloom,	<u>such as never existed in ages past</u>
a day of clouds and total darkness,	<u>and never will again</u>
like the dawn spreading over the mountains;	<u>in all the generations to come.</u>
a great and strong people appears,	

This event that is happening to the people of Israel is unlike anything that has happened to them before. This will be a first-time deal and a last time appointment. Alert, danger is at the door! There is darkness, and an army is headed our way.

There is a first time for everything. Destruction is not always familiar. Destruction changes as we change, and as we start to grow comfortable, destruction comes and reminds us that we are in a fallen world. Destruction is sometimes present to keep believers on their toes and to remind them not to get comfortable, because this is not our home. Our comfort and glory are in the next life. Destruction will forever change so that you can never really get used to it. That is why it is called destruction, because it destroys everything it touches. If you saw destruction coming, it would mean you would have time to prepare, and unfortunately, that is not the case.

CHALLENGE

Today, in the face of destruction say, I see you and I'm not afraid of you because I know who I belong to.

Pray with me: LORD you are good, and you are God. I surrender to your LOVE. I no longer fear the destruction that you allow to come into my life. I no longer fear the hurt or pain. God Give me the strength to lean into your army to be able to lean into your LOVE. Keep me strong LORD. AMEN

YOUR REfLECTIONS:

3 A fire devours in front of them,

and behind them a flame blazes.

The land in front of them

is like the garden of Eden,

but behind them,

it is like a desert wasteland;

there is no escape from them.

4 Their appearance is like that of horses,

and they gallop like war horses.

5 They bound on the tops of the mountains.

Their sound is like the sound of chariots,

like the sound of fiery flames consuming stubble,

like a mighty army deployed for war.

VERSE 3

3 <u>A fire devours in front of them,</u>

<u>and behind them a flame blazes.</u>

The land in front of them

is like the garden of Eden,

but behind them,

it is like a desert wasteland;

there is no escape from them.

A great and powerful army has appeared in the land of Israel, and the army is destructive. In their path fire is destroying everything in front of it, and behind it, and the land is left in ruins. What can the bible of God do at this time? This is the Day of the LORD, and this will be the destructive capabilities of the army.

In life and in our destruction, it can almost seem like wherever we have been, there has always been destruction and chaos. The Day of the LORD is fierce, who can withstand it. In the destruction, things maybe bad, however there is order in the chaos.

CHALLENGE

There is order in the chaos of life. Today in your chaos or your destruction, I challenge you to try to find the order in your chaos. When you find the order in the chaos, this is where you will see the hand of God.

YOUR REFLECTIONS:

VERSE 3

3 A fire devours in front of them,

and behind them a flame blazes.

The land in front of them

is like the garden of Eden,

but behind them,

it is like a desert wasteland;

there is no escape from them.

The destruction of this army is unmatched. A visual is given to show how the Day of the LORD will come. It will happen in transition. Things will slowly start to change, and once everything changes, it will be too late to turn back. The visual that is given is of the garden of Eden. A transition from spiritual prosperity and peace and growth, and ultimately, a close relationship with God in paradise, changes to a spiritually dead dry desert and wasteland.

Destruction can transition us from a place of spiritual paradise to a spiritually dead wasteland. This only happens when we neglect the signs of the LORD. Whatever the means of the destruction, the LORD is still in control of the transition. Fire does not only destroy, but it also heals and helps create life.

CHALLENGE

Look. Did you see it? Did you see the transition from life to death into life again? Today look for where there was death present, but now life is reigning even more.

YOUR REFLECTIONS:

VERSE 3

3 A fire devours in front of them,

and behind them a flame blazes.

The land in front of them

is like the garden of Eden,

but behind them,

it is like a desert wasteland;

there is no escape from them.

Such beautiful words. There is no escape from them. Some may say that I am optimistic, but I see the beauty in this text. There is no hiding from the Day of the LORD. There is no fear of missing out. Every eye will see him. There is no fear of missing out because there Is no escaping his wrath.

The transitions that the LORD draws upon our lives are for our benefit. They are to shape and mold us. We cannot say to the potter why did you let this happen, or why did you create me this way? He makes all things work for the God of those who trust and LOVE him. There is no escaping the Love of the Father and that is a Good thing.

CHALLENGE
Do not try to run from it. Do not try to hide from it. Welcome the Day of the LORD. Welcome the destruction that the LORD provides us to understand and grow as His people.

YOUR REfLECTIONS:

VERSE 4

4 Their appearance is like that of horses,

and they gallop like war horses.

During bible times horses were seen as vehicles of war. Whenever a horse was seen or talked about, this was a sign that war was on the horizon. War was about to happen. This army being compared to horses, and more specifically, war horses tells the people of Israel that there will be war upon war. Prepare for battle. Prepare for the fight of your life.

When we see the signs of war, some will prepare to go into battle. Others will try and find a safe place for shelter, and others will be caught in the crossfire. If war is on the horizon, what will your plans be?

CHALLENGE
Today, plan a war preparation kit or list. And add PRAYER, LOVE, HOPE, AND PEACE to that kit or list, and you should have no worries in the coming war.

YOUR REflECTIONS:

VERSE 5
5 <u>They bound on the tops of the mountains.</u>

Their sound is like the sound of chariots,

like the sound of fiery flames consuming stubble,

like a mighty army deployed for war.

They are running with leaping strides. That is what it means to bound. They are moving in such a way that it looks as if they are leaping from top to top of all the mountains. This attests to the strength and might of the LORD's army.

The man of war is at your door, and his strength is unmatched. What is man to do? There is only one thing we can do when we are outmatched. Surrender. Surrender to the power of the LORD and let God be God. That includes letting Him be the God over your destruction.

CHALLENGE
Have you seen the power of God yet? If not, look for it and when you find it, Surrender. All of creation testifies to God's magnificent strength.

YOUR REFLECTIONS:

VERSE 5
5 They bound on the tops of the mountains.

Their sound is like the sound of chariots,

like the sound of fiery flames consuming stubble,

like a mighty army deployed for war.

The sound alone makes the army mighty. Their mere presence is like the sound of tens of thousands of chariots. The vastness of God's power. This is not only the sound of a mighty army, but it is also, the vision of a mighty army. The image of a fiery flame consuming stubble is terrifying because stubble is simply cut stocks of grain that is left sticking out of the ground after harvest. The land has already been decimated and now the army is burning what is left. This is power and destruction in one sentence.

Want to know what receiving a kick while you are down looks and feels like? Imagine an army burning the very crops they had just destroyed moments earlier. This can and does hurt. However bad things may seem, the LORD is still in control.

CHALLENGE
Have you ever felt like life just kept kicking you while you were down? See that pain and welcome it. I understand that this is easier said than done, however, I believe that God wants you to break through your pain by literally bringing you through the fire. Fire is hot for a reason.

Pray with me: LORD you are good, and you are God. I surrender to your LOVE. The wars may come but I will rest in you. Devastation will come but I will rest in you. Open my eyes so that I may see your blessings in the lesson of destruction.

YOUR REfLECTIONS:

6 Nations writhe in horror before them;

all faces turn pale.

7 They attack as warriors attack;

they scale walls as men of war do.

Each goes on his own path,

and they do not change their course.

8 They do not push each other;

each proceeds on his own path.

They dodge the arrows, never stopping.

9 They storm the city;

they run on the wall;

they climb into the houses;

they enter through the windows like thieves.

10 The earth quakes before them;

the sky shakes.

The sun and moon grow dark,

and the stars cease their shining.

11 The Lord makes his voice heard

in the presence of his army.

His camp is very large;

those who carry out his command are powerful.

Indeed, the day of the Lord is terrible and dreadful—

who can endure it?

VERSE 6
6 Nations writhe in horror before them;

all faces turn pale.

Now, we get a detailed description of the army of the LORD, their might and ability to destroy villages, countries, and nations. The general is the LORD. They fight at the hand of God. Who can stand against them?

The faces of the people who come across the LORD's army are not a pretty sight. Faces turning pale are a sign of extreme fright. This is all truly due to the great army of God. Those that are bold enough to not run in fear will soon be mulled over.

CHALLENGE
The faces of the LORD'S enemies are pale with fright. Be encouraged today that the same army the LORD sends to judge His people, can also be there to encourage His people.

YOUR REFLECTIONS:

VERSE 7

7 They attack as warriors attack;

they scale walls as men of war do.

Each goes on his own path,

and they do not change their course.

The army of the LORD is precise. There is nothing that can stand in the army's path. Every step is calculated. Entire counties and villages have been laid out to survey every possible attack point. After understanding the mission, they attack with precision and power.

What enables this army to move with such precision? They are moving with power down to every remaining detail. We must be reminded that this is the LORD's army. Our God is a god of order, everything has its purpose, and everything is worked out down to the very last detail. God operates in Order. There is no destruction that can come into your life that God has not allowed or ordered for His name sake.

CHALLENGE
In your destruction there is order, the person who has it under control is God. Today rest easy in the hand of God for He has everything in order.

YOUR REFLECTIONS:

VERSE 8

8 They do not push each other;

each proceeds on his own path.

They dodge the arrows, never stopping.

Such control, such focus, such power! The army of God is focused on the mission. They have their orders and now it is time to execute. There is no one that is going rogue. There is no one who will jeopardize the mission. The only focus is to conquer and complete the mission as the LORD has commanded.

We often forget the mission that the LORD has set us on. We forget that He has called us to trust Him and to come to Him with every need. Most importantly to preach the gospel and represent Him to the world. We often forget. Destruction will come, it is coming, it is already here. Remain faithful to the mission and remain faithful to God.

CHALLENGE

Have you strayed away from the mission? Have you forgotten your purpose? Today, pray and realign your self to what God has called you to do regardless of the destruction around you.

YOUR REFLECTIONS:

VERSE 9
9 They storm the city;

they run on the wall;

they climb into the houses;

they enter through the windows like thieves.

They storm the city and run up and down walls, and they are able to enter the house as a thief. These are skills that take years of training to be able to execute flawlessly. Yet, the army of the LORD is ready and are executing the task as the LORD commanded. When did God have time to train them? When did he take time aside to recruit the best of the best? The answer, He is God and He only has the best of the best.

God has a well-trained army. What does that mean for us? He provided the training for such an army, and the testing facilities to see what would work and what would not. He had the funding to supply all the army's needs. Are you a child of God? If so, then he has provided everything you need for success in this life.

CHALLENGE
God had provided everything that His army needed for their success. The same goes for you. He has provided everything you need for your successes. You simply need to walk in your training.

YOUR REFLECTIONS:

VERSE 10
10 The earth quakes before them;

the sky shakes.

The sun and moon grow dark,

and the stars cease their shining.

Amazing power for an amazing army. As they take a step, the earth shakes. As they run, the earth trembles under their feet. The sun turns dark, and the moon no longer has any light to reflect, so it too goes dark. All in the presence of the mighty army of the LORD.

Imagine taking a step and feeling the ground shake under your feet. Imagine stepping outside only to have the sun go dark in your presence. This my friend is the power of authority that the army of God has. You also have an authority that you must walk in. You are a child of God. The same God who has such an army, yes Him, you are his son.

CHALLENGE
Have you been walking in the authority God has given you? Remember who your father is. You are His son Walk in His authority as His son or daughter.

YOUR REFLECTIONS:

VERSE 11
11 The Lord makes his voice heard

in the presence of his army.

His camp is very large;

those who carry out his command are powerful.

Indeed, the day of the Lord is terrible and
dreadful—

who can endure it?

The army brings terror to people. The army moves with such precision. The same army is skilled and ready for war. The earth trembles under their feet. They are focused on what the mission is, and nothing can stand in their way. This mighty army is under the hand of God. The magnificent army can do nothing if the LORD God does not allow them to do so. This is the power of God.

The army is powerful, but they listen to the voice of God. As big as this army is, it can destroy whole nations, yet it is controlled by God. No matter your circumstance in life, it still yields to the voice of the LORD. No matter how strong the destruction or how painful it may be, it still must obey the LORD.

CHALLENGE
The army is under the control of the LORD. It is not just the army, but all things are under the control of the LORD. Your pain is under the control of the LORD. Whatever your hurt or struggle, it is under the control of the LORD.

Pray with me: LORD, You are good, and You are God. God, Your army is Big; however, it is under Your control. Thank You LORD for showing me even the biggest things in the world are under Your control. AMEN

YOUR REflECTIONS:

12 Even now—

this is the Lord's declaration—

turn to me with all your heart,

with fasting, weeping, and mourning.

13 Tear your hearts,

not just your clothes,

and return to the Lord your God.

For he is gracious and compassionate,

slow to anger, abounding in faithful love,

and he relents from sending disaster.

14 Who knows? He may turn and relent

and leave a blessing behind him,

so you can offer a grain offering and a drink offering

to the Lord your God.

VERSE 12
12 Even now—

this is the Lord's declaration—

turn to me with all your heart,

with fasting, weeping, and mourning.

While the army of the LORD is at the door of the Israelites, He calls them to repent. While destruction is at their heels, they are told to turn to God. Oh, what a mighty God we serve. He calls them to turn to Him with everything they have. That is what turning to God with all your heart means. It means your very being. That is what he is asking of His people, and He gives them instructions on how to do it.

To turn to God with all your heart seems like a daunting task, however God always gives instructions on how to follow Him. This act of repentance is done by fasting, weeping, and mourning. In fasting, weeping, and mourning, you are to be operating in a state of grief and loss. It is this mindset that brings a person to full repentance.

CHALLENGE
Who would have thought that even amid destruction, God still calls His people to repent? Have you done so? If not, I recommend starting with a fast.

YOUR REFLECTIONS:

VERSE 13

13 <u>Tear your hearts,</u>

<u>not just your clothes,</u>

<u>and return to the Lord your God.</u>

For he is gracious and compassionate,

slow to anger, abounding in faithful love,

and he relents from sending disaster.

Now the instructions go a little deeper. In times of fasting, often the heart was not into the submission of fasting. When they would fast, they would tear their clothes to show how sorry they were, but their hearts remained the same. God has noticed this and called them to do better.

To tear your heart not just your clothes, called for the inward looking of what is the root of the sin. We often sin and sin and sin and continue to say I am sorry God. Now He calls us to look at our hearts to see what the real issue may be. In finding the heart of the problem, we are able to truly repent and break habits that were drawing us away from God.

CHALLENGE

What is the root of the problem? Have you looked inside to see the cause? Today, reflect on your habitual sin and try to find where the source lies.

YOUR REFLECTIONS:

VERSE 13

13 Tear your hearts,

not just your clothes,

and return to the Lord your God.

For he is gracious and compassionate,

slow to anger, abounding in faithful love,

and he relents from sending disaster.

The Israelites had to understand who God is. We must remember the army is still at the door. God calls them to repent and now there is a possible response from God. This is not from the hope of the people but more so from the character of God. They are hoping to see this character trait of God come forth.

In searching our hearts, we will see that God is sympathetic to us. His grace is enough for you and me. His sympathy and concern for you is the basis of His love for mankind. We must remind ourselves that He is gracious and compassionate.

CHALLENGE

Your situation does not change the character of God. He is the same yesterday, today, and forever. However, we also must get to the place where we fully recognize the God we serve. Today, think and pray on how God has been gracious and compassionate to you. You may find the storm is not that bad.

YOUR REFLECTIONS:

VERSE 13
13 Tear your hearts,

not just your clothes,

and return to the Lord your God.

For he is gracious and compassionate,

<u>slow to anger, abounding in faithful love,</u>

and he relents from sending disaster.

The characteristics of God continue. The prophet now acknowledges that God is slow to anger and faithful in His Love. The slow to anger is only possible through God's faithful love. The Israelites are to rely on God's faithful love for them to slow His anger. The anger is there but that does not change the fact that God still loves His people.

Yes, give us the God who doesn't get angry with us, give us the God who loves us no matter what. That my friend, is not the God of the Bible. We must understand that God does hate sin and wants no part of it. However, he has a love for us that is so big, He sent his son to die for us, to cover the very sin he hates.

CHALLENGE
Understand that God hates your sin but do know that He loves you. Today, pray on the times where God was slow to anger with you, and you will see his faithful love for you.

YOUR REflECTIONS:

VERSE 13

13 Tear your hearts,

not just your clothes,

and return to the Lord your God.

For he is gracious and compassionate,

slow to anger, abounding in faithful love,

<u>and he relents from sending disaster.</u>

This is what the Israelites are hoping. They are hoping that God would relent from sending disaster on them. This is possible. God has done more with worse. However, the only thing that can fulfill such a request is the broken spirit and contrite heart of His people.

We often want God to take the pain away. We want him to get rid of everything that is bringing us down, yet our hearts remain unchanged. We must first be willing to change our hearts before we can approach the throne of Grace.

CHALLENGE

What have you done that you feel should make God relent from sending disaster? We are all sinners. The very fact that we are breathing is through the grace of God. God relents on His own accord. Our submission helps us understand his grace. Be thankful.

YOUR REFLECTIONS:

VERSE 14
14 Who knows? He may turn and relent

and leave a blessing behind him,

so you can offer a grain offering and a drink offering

to the Lord your God.

Who knows, the lord may turn and relent. The Israelites did not know what the outcome would be in their submission to the LORD. All they knew was that they should be obedient and trust God. The outcome of the obedience is a possible blessing.

In total submission, God will always provide a way for his people to worship Him. In our submission that we reach when we fast and turn our hearts unto the LORD, He provides enough for us to bring an offering to the throne.

CHALLENGE
Today praise God in your offering. Praise God in your suffering. He will always leave enough for us to worship and praise Him. Sometimes the reason is He is God and God alone.

Pray with me: LORD, You are good, and You are God. God, You continue to provide a blessing in the destruction, thus I will worship you in the storm. AMEN

YOUR REflECTIONS:

15 Blow the ram's horn in Zion!

Announce a sacred fast;

proclaim a solemn assembly.

16 Gather the people;

sanctify the congregation;

assemble the aged;

gather the infants,

even babies nursing at the breast.

Let the groom leave his bedroom,

and the bride her honeymoon chamber.

17 Let the priests, the Lord's ministers,

weep between the portico and the altar.

Let them say,

"Have pity on your people, Lord,

and do not make your inheritance a disgrace,

an object of scorn among the nations.

Why should it be said among the peoples,

'Where is their God?'"

VERSE 15
15 Blow the ram's horn in Zion!

Announce a sacred fast;

proclaim a solemn assembly.

This is the second time where we see a cry out for a return to the LORD. The first time was during the Plague of Locust. This time it is the coming day of the LORD. The army of God is about to wipe out Israel, and the hope of the people of God is a sacred fast. Everyone must be made aware of this petition to the LORD.

It is quite encouraging to see the people of God going to Him amid their troubles. This is the second time they are running to Him and He is not tired of it. There is no set limit of how many times you can come to God with your problems. He has ears to hear and arms that can save.

CHALLENGE
Have you felt like you were bothering God with your constant prayer request? Or your constant groaning and moaning out to Him? Do understand that He loves it when you cry out to him. Today, don't let up. Continue to cry out to God.

YOUR REFLECTIONS:

VERSE 16

16 <u>Gather the people;</u>	Let the groom leave his bedroom,
<u>sanctify the congregation;</u>	and the bride her honeymoon chamber.
<u>assemble the aged;</u>	
<u>gather the infants,</u>	
<u>even babies nursing at the breast.</u>	

Alert everyone, no one should be left out. If they were created in the image of God, they are to be a part of this sacred assembly. They are to set themselves apart holy to the LORD obeying his every command. No one is too young to start submitting to the LORD.

The people are to come in the presence of the LORD ready to surrender all and be accountable for their sin. They were to come broken and willing to submit to the Law of the LORD. Everyone was to be included in this assembly.

CHALLENGE
Do you have brothers or sisters you can call upon to go with you before the LORD? If so, call them and ask them to labor with you as you go before the LORD. If you do not have anyone you can call upon, stop what you are doing and seek after those who LOVE the LORD as much as you and who are willing to walk with you.

YOUR REFLECTIONS:

VERSE 16

16 Gather the people;

sanctify the congregation;

assemble the aged;

gather the infants,

even babies nursing at the breast.

Let the groom leave his bedroom,

and the bride her honeymoon chamber.

The groom is to relieve himself of his marital duties, and the wife hers, so that they may go before the LORD broken and contrite. This was how the bonding of the two was consummated. The marriage was sealed on the wedding night thus establishing the union of the couple. This was a covenant.

This is a beautiful picture of the faithfulness to God over everything. Yes, the wedding night is important. Yes, the covenant must be sealed, however the covenant means nothing if the covenant before God is not honored. We must seek to honor God first before we seek to honor anything else in life and that includes loved ones.

CHALLENGE

Your covenants are a small 2 of hearts compared to God's ace of spades. His covenant goes first before all things. Today ask yourself, who is holding the trump card? You or God. Look at your life to find out.

YOUR REFLECTIONS:

VERSE 17

17 <u>Let the priests, the Lord's ministers, weep between the portico and the altar.</u>

Let them say,

"Have pity on your people, Lord,

and do not make your inheritance a disgrace,

an object of scorn among the nations.

Why should it be said among the peoples,

'Where is their God?'"

Once again, we see the place of the priest and the men of God. They know their place and know what must be done. They must lead the people of God because it is on them that all eyes are on. If they fail to lead, the people of Israel are lost, because they are one of the voices of God to the people.

The priest knows the role that they must play in this sacred assembly. They must show in their own lives their trust and dependence on God. The people should model what they see. You must be willing to come and weep at the altar of the LORD when you recognize you have been missing the mark.

CHALLENGE
How willing are you to go to the altar of the LORD once you realize you are in sin? How long does it take for you to make that first step? Do you simply say LORD forgive me, or do you come to God broken in your sin?

YOUR REFLECTIONS:

VERSE 17

17 Let the priests, the Lord's ministers, weep between the portico and the altar.

Let them say,

"Have pity on your people, Lord,

and do not make your inheritance a disgrace,

an object of scorn among the nations.

Why should it be said among the peoples,

'Where is their God?'"

Now we have the confession and plea of the people of God. There is an admission of guilt (Have pity on your people, Lord) and then there is an ask for forgiveness. The Priest calls on the characteristics of God as a plea to stand before them. They call themselves as the inheritance of God.

You must remind yourself who you are to God. God already knows who you are to Him. Often, we forget that we are his children and He calls us friends. Nothing can separate us from His love for His children.

CHALLENGE

Today, look at yourself in the mirror and say who you are in the eyes of God.

YOUR REflECTIONS:

VERSE 17

17 Let the priests, the Lord's ministers, weep between the portico and the altar.

Let them say,

"Have pity on your people, Lord,

and do not make your inheritance a disgrace,

an object of scorn among the nations.

<u>Why should it be said among the peoples,</u>

<u>'Where is their God?'"</u>

Such a bold statement. Why should the people of the earth say, "where is their God?" The priest of Israel knew. If God did not act, they would be annihilated and the surrounding nations would say, hmmm, their God abandoned them and left them to be destroyed. This was the fear. They were in this place of fear to be left without a God

Sometimes our sins can be so heavy that we think that God is not with us. That he has left us alone and has turned in his resignation on being our God. This is a lie from the enemy. God is ever present. It is less about God leaving us than it is about our sin pulling us away from God.

CHALLENGE

Your sin may be pulling you away from God. Now is the time to call upon God to act and save you.

Pray with me: LORD you are good, and you are God. God save me from my sin. It pulls me and distracts me from your love and your constant presence in my life. God I am yours and you are mine. I have been bought with the blood of your Son. I have freedom in you. AMEN

YOUR REfLECTIONS:

18 Then the Lord became jealous

for his land and spared his people.

19 The Lord answered his people:

Look, I am about to send you

grain, new wine, and fresh oil.

You will be satiated with them,

and I will no longer make you

a disgrace among the nations.

20 I will drive the northerner far
from you

and banish him to a dry and desolate
land,

his front ranks into the Dead Sea,

and his rear guard into the
Mediterranean Sea.

His stench will rise;

yes, his rotten smell will rise,

for he has done astonishing things.

VERSE 18
18 Then the Lord became jealous

for his land and spared his people.

The Lord became jealous for his people. Why would God be jealous? He owns everything in the universe. The jealousy is coming from being fiercely protective or vigilant of one's rights or possessions. In this manner, the LORD is right to get jealous for His people, because they belong to Him. God shows how much He cares about the people of Israel through this act of jealousy.

God spares his people, not because they are perfect, but because they cried out for Him to save them. Often, we fail to cry out for the Lord to save us. When we do, we may find that He is very jealous for us just as He is with the people of Israel.

CHALLENGE
Did you know that God is Jealous for you? He is fiercely protective of you, and He loves you. Today, ponder on this jealousy of God and rest in the comfort of His love.

YOUR REFLECTIONS:

VERSE 19
19 <u>The Lord answered his people:</u>

Look, I am about to send you

grain, new wine, and fresh oil.

You will be satiated with them,

and I will no longer make you

a disgrace among the nations.

To sum up all the responses from God in the Bible and for the Bible, we can come up with these five words: the LORD answered His people. God answers those who cry out for Him. He answers those who pray to Him and ask of Him.

The LORD is ever listening, and He is ever present. His ears are perked, and they are ready to listen to your every cry. He calls us to pray, so as faithful children we must pray.

CHALLENGE
Today, do something you have never done before. Today pray for every decision of your day. To choose soda or water, Go to the LORD in prayer. To use salt or pepper, Go to the LORD in prayer. The LORD is listening, and you will get through the day.

YOUR REFLECTIONS:

VERSE 19

19 The Lord answered his people:

Look, I am about to send you

grain, new wine, and fresh oil.

You will be satiated with them,

and I will no longer make you

a disgrace among the nations.

The LORD is about to do something amazing for the people of Israel. We have already established that the land is destroyed. How is the LORD going to provide grain, new wine, and fresh oil? The LORD God is planning on restoring the land of the people of Israel. The grass will grow, and the olive trees will bare fruit for the people of God.

The LORD answered the people of Israel. Why did he answer them? Because they prayed to Him. Now He goes into detail on how He will restore His people, and how they will be able to go back to the altar and worship Him.

CHALLENGE

The LORD is going to restore you, your land, and your hope. Today, be encouraged in His word and rest knowing you serve a God who restores.

YOUR REFLECTIONS:

VERSE 19
19 The Lord answered his people:

Look, I am about to send you

grain, new wine, and fresh oil.

You will be satiated with them,

and I will no longer make you

a disgrace among the nations.

God tells the people that they will be fully satisfied with what He is about to bring. Here the LORD does not simply provide food, but He provides an abundance of food, grain, and wine. The LORD continues to promise the people of Israel that He will no longer make them a disgrace. He will be their grace. And they will never be too far from His grace. He will take them from being without grace to dwelling with grace.

God plans on restoring His grace to His people. They will not be far from his LOVE. Their needs will be met, and their hearts will be at peace with their God.

CHALLENGE
God longs to satisfy those who cry out to Him. Will you cry out today?

YOUR REFLECTIONS:

VERSE 20

20 I will drive the northerner far from you

and banish him to a dry and desolate land,

his front ranks into the Dead Sea,

and his rear guard into the Mediterranean Sea.

His stench will rise;

yes, his rotten smell will rise,

for he has done astonishing things.

How will God provide the increase if the invader is still in the land? When God answers, He answers fully, nothing is left out. God knew His people wanted food and oil for worship. He knew they wanted relief from the invaders. God knew, and he provided for His people. Part of God providing for His people is God himself removing the hindrances in their lives.

Part of God providing is removing the obstacles in our lives. For God to fully provide for our every need, we need to be willing to break free from those that draw us away from the LORD. Sometimes we are the obstacle, it is ourselves that we need to surrender who we are to the LORD.

CHALLENGE

Today, find those obstacles that need to be driven out of your life. This maybe a friend or member of your family and it might even be you. Whatever it is, surrender it to the LORD.

YOUR REFLECTIONS:

VERSE 20

20 I will drive the northerner far from you

and banish him to a dry and desolate land,

his front ranks into the Dead Sea,

and his rear guard into the Mediterranean Sea.

His stench will rise;

yes, his rotten smell will rise,

for he has done astonishing things.

Why have emphasis on the stench of the invader? Why describe the smell? When an offering was done to the LORD, if the LORD accepted the offering, he would call it a pleasing aroma. If the offering was not received, the consequences would be dire. The sacrificial offering would not be pleasing to the Lord. The people were the cause of the invaders and for them to restore their relationship with the LORD, they would need to humble themselves and offer it unto the LORD. The stench of the smell shows that the LORD wanted nothing to do with the people of Israel's idolatry.

Your offering that has been pulling you away from the LORD is ready to be sacrificed. This will not be pleasing to the LORD because it is not the offering the LORD is looking for, but you.

CHALLENGE

Today offer up the reason for your drifting from the LORD and surrender it to HIM.

Pray with me: LORD you are good, and you are God. God, my sin against you is heavy and I cannot carry it. Lead me and show me where in my life I have strayed from You and let me bring it to Your altar. Please forgive me. God give me the heart to release my hands to Your LOVE. AMEN

YOUR REFLECTIONS:

21 Don't be afraid, land;

rejoice and be glad,

for the Lord has done astonishing things.

22 Don't be afraid, wild animals,

for the wilderness pastures have turned green,

the trees bear their fruit,

and the fig tree and grapevine yield their riches.

23 Children of Zion, rejoice and be glad

in the Lord your God,

because he gives you the autumn rain

for your vindication.

He sends showers for you,

both autumn and spring rain as before.

24 The threshing floors will be full of grain,

and the vats will overflow

with new wine and fresh oil.

VERSE 21
21 Don't be afraid, land;

rejoice and be glad,

for the Lord has done astonishing things.

The land that once grieved is now rejoicing in the LORD. When God restores, He restores everything. He calls the Land to rejoice and be glad because He has done amazing things. The astonishing things are the LORD driving out the hindrances of growth. This gives the land the joy to be glad in the LORD.

This same land was once grieving. It was crying out to the LORD. It was dry and could not rejoice in its barren surroundings. However, God brought life to the land. If God is restoring the land and calling it to rejoice, surely, He can restore us and call us to rejoice.

CHALLENGE
He is restoring creation, and you are included in such a restoration. Today, thank God for His restorative powers.

YOUR REFLECTIONS:

VERSE 22
22 Don't be afraid, wild animals,

for the wilderness pastures have turned green,

the trees bear their fruit,

and the fig tree and grapevine yield their riches.

The pastures and fruit are no longer dried up. They are no longer withered. They bare their fruit in their season and in their time. They are not only living, but they are thriving. So much so, He calls the wild animals to come and eat. The land has produced fresh grass, and the trees are dropping their fruit. He calls creation to come and taste and see how the LORD is good.

Don't be afraid He tells the wild animals. What should they fear? The fear of hunger is the fear. He tells them not to fear hunger, because he has restored the land and the land is rejoicing and now it is time for the creatures of the earth to have their fill. It makes sense that He would call the land before the creatures; He did in fact create the land first.

CHALLENGE
Do not be afraid. Your time is coming. There is a process and your spot has not been overlooked. Trust God and be patient. He called the land first, then the animals, you are next.

YOUR REFLECTIONS:

VERSE 23
23 Children of Zion, rejoice and be glad

in the Lord your God,

because he gives you the autumn rain

for your vindication.

He sends showers for you,

both autumn and spring rain as before.

First the land, then the animals, now it is time for the children of God. It is our time to shine and be restored. He calls them to be glad and rejoice, because He has brought the rain upon his people. The rain brings life, healing and produce. The rain also washes away our dirt and sin. The people of God are now clear of their guilt.

We have been vindicated by the blood of Christ. He has restored and brought about complete healing. Those same rains that God brought on His people are a symbol of God washing His people clean and restoring and bringing life to them. Rest in the rain of God

CHALLENGE
Be glad, it is now our turn to be restored. Go out into the rain of God and let Him wash you clean.

YOUR REFLECTIONS:

VERSE 23

23 Children of Zion, rejoice and be glad

in the Lord your God,

because he gives you the autumn rain

for your vindication.

He sends showers for you,

both autumn and spring rain as before.

Things are back in order. He is now giving His people a double portion of what they have been missing. The rain will not only come in the spring but also in the autumn. This calls for a bigger harvest at the end of the year. God is now providing provisions for His people.

For the Israelites, their double portion came in the way of rain for more crops. Our double portion may be different. For some it may be more rain in our lives to further wash everything away. For others, it may be having more of what you lost in your destruction. Whatever it may be, God is restoring and is providing double for what you have lost in this life or in the next.

CHALLENGE

When you are in the season of your double portion, be surrendered to receive all that the LORD has for you. Seek first His kingdom.

YOUR REfLECTIONS:

VERSE 24
24 <u>The threshing floors will be full of grain,</u>

and the vats will overflow

with new wine and fresh oil.

In their sin, the farmers had to be ashamed, because they did not store enough grain during the famine and invasion. Now their shame is gone. God not only restores the land and the grain, but also the shame of those who were broken during the famine. The floors are full of grain because of the blessing of the LORD.

God restores not only the physical but also the spiritual and the psychological. The shame that once had the farmers down, now God has filled with hope and prosperity. There is no more shame for those who repent and turn to the LORD.

CHALLENGE
Today, walk out of your shame that came with the destruction in your life. God has restored you.

YOUR REFLECTIONS:

VERSE 24
24 The threshing floors will be full of grain,

and the vats will overflow

with new wine and fresh oil.

The vats that were once dried up are now overflowing with a new spirit and new wine. The spirit of the LORD has been poured out afresh onto the people of Israel. Their cup is now running over. In their repentance, they are filled with the spirit and restored and refilled by the grace of God.

The spirit is poured on the people of God. With new oil and new wine, we are able to walk in the newness of LIFE.

CHALLENGE
Today, ask for an outpouring of the new oil and wine over your life.

Pray with me: LORD You are good, and You are God. God restore me and bring me back to my perfection in creation. Let me walk ever fearing You and You alone, and may my hope be in You. AMEN

YOUR REFLECTIONS:

25 I will repay you for the years

that the swarming locust ate,

the young locust, the destroying locust,

and the devouring locust—

my great army that I sent against you.

26 You will have plenty to eat and be satisfied.

You will praise the name of the Lord your God,

who has dealt wondrously with you.

My people will never again be put to shame.

27 You will know that I am present in Israel

and that I am the Lord your God,

and there is no other.

My people will never again be put to shame.

VERSE 25
25 I will repay you for the years

that the swarming locust ate,

the young locust, the destroying locust,

and the devouring locust—

my great army that I sent against you.

The LORD is repaying the people of Israel for the destruction that was sent upon them. He is restoring what was once lost and destroyed. He first claims the swarming locust. The swarming locust represents the destruction that moved as one and that conquered the people of Israel.

This same destruction that came into your life rapidly, and subsequently, bad things kept happening one after the other. This was the swarm of destruction that was mentioned previously in pages past. The best way to get out of a swarm is to treat it like a storm; you drive through it. Press through the storm. God is waiting on the other side with restoration and peace.

CHALLENGE
God is repaying and restoring for what the swarming locust has eaten. Look at your life today and see where he has brought you through the storm and healed you.

YOUR REflECTIONS:

VERSE 25
25 I will repay you for the years

that the swarming locust ate,

the young locust, the destroying locust,

and the devouring locust—

my great army that I sent against you.

The destruction that came from inexperience is now being conquered by experience. God is covering all bases for His people. The young and immature habits of unbelief are now over. There has been growth for the people of God.

What the young locust brought with them was the error of lack of experience. As we face trials in life, we never truly face them twice. When we have gone through a trial, we come out on the other side more mature and prepared to face the same or similar trial with far greater success than previously.

CHALLENGE
Your weakness in your former trial is now your confidence in your current trial. Trust God and He will help you.

YOUR REflECTIONS:

VERSE 25
25 I will repay you for the years

that the swarming locust ate,

the young locust, the destroying locust,

and the devouring locust—

my great army that I sent against you.

Oh, how the hand of the LORD rebuilds. The destroying locust came and wiped out the people of God. Yet God is able to restore. What was broken is now together. What was sick is now healed. What was destroyed is now in order.

Where destruction has come over your life, God has provided healing for such a time. There is new growth in the hand of the Father, and there is understanding in a world of chaos. The God that allowed the locust to come is the same God that causes the grass to grow in season.

CHALLENGE
Hope, there is hope for you. There is peace for you. There is a God who loves you. Seek Him today.

YOUR REFLECTIONS:

Week Twelve-Day 4

VERSE 25
25 I will repay you for the years

that the swarming locust ate,

the young locust, the destroying locust,

and the devouring locust—

my great army that I sent against you.

Who sent the army? Who allowed this army to come and mess up the life of the Israelites? God. God sent the army. He sent the devouring locust to his people, and the locust destroyed them swiftly. Destruction came upon them like a thief in the night. They never saw it coming.

Why would God send such a terrible army against His people? Short answer, they are His people. God is jealous for His Glory and His people. When the people start to give the glory, honor, and praise, that belong to God, to created things, that is when we have a problem. The people turned away from God. He was simply turning them back towards Himself.

CHALLENGE
The Lord allows destruction to come into our lives to draw us closer to the Creator, who is Himself. We often place created things in His place. Worship the Creator today.

YOUR REFLECTIONS:

VERSE 26
26 You will have plenty to eat and be satisfied.

You will praise the name of the Lord your God,

who has dealt wondrously with you.

My people will never again be put to shame.

The LORD now gives His people the opportunity to rejoice. After the trial, the LOVE encourages His people. They are able to rest in His power and in the peace of never again being put to shame. What was once shameful, God has made shameless

The shame you have felt or had for most of your life, God can take it away. Through the pain and the hurt, God still says that He has dealt wondrously with His children. You are his child, and He has dealt wondrously with you. He will remove the shame.

CHALLENGE
Today walk out of your shame that came with the destruction in your life. God has restored you. You are in His hands where there is comfort and peace.

YOUR REflECTIONS:

VERSE 27
27 You will know that I am present in Israel

and that I am the Lord your God,

and there is no other.

My people will never again be put to shame.

God provides evidence for His people. He tells them that they will know that He is God and that He is present. How does he do this? He does this by healing the land. He does this by drawing His people back to Him. He does this by showing His people that he brings peace and that He is the only one who can save His people.

God shows us that He is God every day. From the breaths we take, to waking us up in the morning. Without our acknowledgment, God has saved us from physical harm many times. By His Grace alone we are here. By this alone we should know that He is the LORD.

CHALLENGE
Today reflect on the literal times God has shown you that He is the LORD.

Pray with me: LORD you are good, and you are God. God, thank you for your healing and your restoration. Open my eyes that I may see that you are the LORD and that you are God. AMEN

YOUR REFLECTIONS:

28 After this

I will pour out my Spirit on all humanity;

then your sons and your daughters will prophesy,

your old men will have dreams,

and your young men will see visions.

29 I will even pour out my Spirit

on the male and female slaves in those days.

30 I will display wonders

in the heavens and on the earth:

blood, fire, and columns of smoke.

31 The sun will be turned to darkness

and the moon to blood

before the great and terrible day of the Lord comes.

32 Then everyone who calls

on the name of the Lord will be saved,

for there will be an escape

for those on Mount Zion and in Jerusalem,

as the Lord promised,

among the survivors the Lord calls

Week Thirteen-Day 1

VERSE 28
28 After this

I will pour out my Spirit on all humanity;

then your sons and your daughters will prophesy,

your old men will have dreams,

and your young men will see visions.

After the LORD takes away the shame of His people, He then pours out His Spirit on them. Everyone will be included in this out pouring of the Spirit. Though this is set to happen in the future, it is an encouragement for the people of Israel to trust God in the healing process. His Spirit will fall on the old and the young. There will be no one without the Spirit of the LORD.

When the LORD says that the old men will dream dreams and young men will see visions, He is being active in the young and the old. He will speak to those who are sleeping, and he will also call those who are awake to take action. The LORD will call, and we must be ready to answer.

CHALLENGE
When God takes your shame, He also puts His Spirit in you. Today walk in that Spirit. Part of walking in the Spirit is walking in the word of God.

YOUR REFLECTIONS:

VERSE 29
29 I will even pour out my Spirit

on the male and female slaves in those days.

Those who are in bondage, those who are broken, those who are in chains, even the servant, God will pour out His Spirit. This is to say, there is no one who will miss the outpouring of the Spirit of God. This brings meaning to what Jesus said, "Blessed are the poor for theirs is the kingdom of God." The kingdom of God is theirs. They do not miss out on the goodness of God.

You are never too low that God will not reach down, and grab, and take away your shame. He will take all that is holding you and set you free in His name.

CHALLENGE
Nothing can separate us from the LOVE of God. Part of walking without shame is walking in His promise. Walk in the LORD's promises today.

YOUR REflECTIONS:

VERSE 30
30 I will display wonders

in the heavens and on the earth:

blood, fire, and columns of smoke.

Every eye will see the coming of the LORD and the outpouring of His Spirit. We will see signs and wonders. This will not only come from human hands but also from creation as we know it.

Signs and wonders were often times seen as verifications for people, to prove they were who they said they were. Through these very signs, the people on earth will know that HE is the LORD.

CHALLENGE
How have you seen God work in your life? Have you seen signs and wonders? Today, take time and reflect on these.

YOUR REFLECTIONS:

VERSE 31
31 The sun will be turned to darkness

and the moon to blood

before the great and terrible day of the Lord comes.

Again, we see the submission of creation to the Father. All of creation knows that they are subject to the LORD. In the New Testament the sun turned dark for three hours. In fact, scripture say that darkness fell over the land. This was bigger than a solar eclipse; this was creation bowing down to its Creator as the Son of Man died.

Creation yields to the Father. How hard is it for us to yield to the Father in the morning or the evenings or throughout our day? We must learn from creation to submit to the Creator.

CHALLENGE
When was the last time you yielded to the LORD? Today, yield to Him.

YOUR REFLECTIONS:

VERSE 32

32 <u>Then everyone who calls</u>   as the Lord promised,

<u>on the name of the Lord will be saved,</u>   among the survivors the Lord calls.

for there will be an escape

for those on Mount Zion and in
Jerusalem,

Salvation comes with a repentant heart. Everyone who calls on the name of the
LORD will be saved!

CHALLENGE
Today read these scriptures: Romans 3:23, 6:23, 10:9-10.

YOUR REFLECTIONS:

VERSE 32

32 Then everyone who calls

on the name of the Lord will be saved,

<u>for there will be an escape</u>

<u>for those on Mount Zion and in
Jerusalem,</u>

<u>as the Lord promised,</u>

<u>among the survivors the Lord calls.</u>

Salvation comes to those who repent. Part of repenting is confessing your sin to the LORD specifically. He provides the escape for His people in His coming day. He called the people to run to Him for their salvation. This call is not different for us now.

Terror is on the horizon, and you have the opportunity to chase God and run to Him, for salvation will you come?

CHALLENGE

Today, ask yourself did you run, and will you run?

Pray with me: LORD you are good, and you are God. God, thank you for your saving grace. Thank you for providing a way out for me. I long to be in your presence as I seek refuge in your name. AMEN

YOUR REfLECTIONS:

1 Yes, in those days and at that time,

when I restore the fortunes of Judah and Jerusalem,

2 I will gather all the nations

and take them to the Valley of Jehoshaphat.

I will enter into judgment with them there

because of my people, my inheritance Israel.

The nations have scattered the Israelites

in foreign countries

and divided up my land.

3 They cast lots for my people;

they bartered a boy for a prostitute

and sold a girl for wine to drink.

4 And also: Tyre, Sidon, and all the territories of Philistia—what are you to me?

Are you paying me back or trying to get even with me?

I will quickly bring retribution on your heads

VERSE 1

1 Yes, in those days and at that time,

when I restore the fortunes of Judah and Jerusalem,

In those days when God will restore and save His people, He will also restore the earth. This was a promise to the people of Israel. This is the future coming of the day of the LORD. It has not happened yet. He is telling them what will happen in the future. In these words, the people of Israel are encouraged.

There is a plan that God is working that we may not see, but he will make clear soon in the end. We must trust that when He says He will restore; He will restore everything.

CHALLENGE

The restoration does not stop with your healing, but it continues with the healing of all things around you. Walk in this healing today.

YOUR Reflections:

VERSE 2

2 I will gather all the nations

and take them to the Valley of Jehoshaphat.

I will enter into judgment with them there

because of my people, my inheritance Israel.

The nations have scattered the Israelites in foreign countries

and divided up my land.

Part of restoring is removing the hindrances around Israel. God promises that He will also gather and judge all the other nations. This is the sign of the total restoration of the earth. A set place and a set time for the judgment of the LORD.

It is not only your immediate surroundings that the LORD will heal, but those that surround you and beyond. God plans on judging all the nations of the earth. In those nations are people, pray for the hearts that are not towards the LORD.

CHALLENGE

Today, pray for those in other nations. Pray for your family and friends who do not know the LORD that they may come to know Him and feel His peace.

YOUR REFLECTIONS:

VERSE 2

2 I will gather all the nations

and take them to the Valley of Jehoshaphat.

I will enter into judgment with them there

because of my people, my inheritance Israel.

The nations have scattered the Israelites

in foreign countries

and divided up my land.

In this context, the judgment that will be on the nations directly affects the nations that are surrounding Israel. God plans on paying them back for attacking, falsely leading, and pulling His people away from Him.

God shows His passion for His people. He remembers and plans on addressing everything that was done to His people Israel. You are blessed for God is also fighting for you. He sees and knows your pain.

CHALLENGE

God restores all. Pray for those who have not experienced His healing. Pray that their eyes maybe open to see the goodness of God.

YOUR REFLECTIONS:

VERSE 2

2 I will gather all the nations

and take them to the Valley of Jehoshaphat.

I will enter into judgment with them there

because of my people, my inheritance Israel.

<u>The nations have scattered the Israelites</u>

<u>in foreign countries</u>

<u>and divided up my land.</u>

The reason for God's judgment toward the nations is His heart, His people. The Father's LOVE remembers and fights for His people. They have transported His people to forging countries, and they have divided up the land of His people. We witness that it was not the people that the invading nations sinned against, but God Himself. For he says, they divided up MY LAND.

When we sin against one another it is not only them that we sin against, but it is God that we sin against. It is He that we should go to seeking repentance. When we confess our sins, He is faithful and just to forgive us.

CHALLENGE

Are you walking in unforgiveness toward someone? Have you taken it to God? Today, bring your sin to Him. He is faithful and Just to forgive us.

YOUR REFLECTIONS:

VERSE 3
3 They cast lots for my people;

they bartered a boy for a prostitute

and sold a girl for wine to drink.

We may ask ourselves, how bad were these nations to the people of God? Here we see the level of sin on His people. They traded youthfulness for pleasure. They traded values of royalty for immediate satisfaction. These were the hearts of the people. They lacked morals. They twisted the value of what was given for pleasure.

Such is the heart of those who do not know God. The hearts of those who do not know God twist scripture and rebel against the Holy Father. We are to pray for those who do not know or see the LORD that their eyes maybe open.

CHALLENGE
Today, pray for those who do not see scripture and God clearly. Pray for eyes to be opened.

YOUR REFLECTIONS:

VERSE 4

4 And also: Tyre, Sidon, and all the territories of
Philistia—what are you to me?

Are you paying me back or trying to get even with me?

I will quickly bring retribution on your heads

How foolish is the man that tries to challenge God? His ways are impure. They waver like the water of the seas. They are broken and try to fix themselves with their own power. This they cannot do for they lack the will and the power. Foolish are they to challenge God. He will bring retribution on their heads.

Do not try to wrestle with God or try to get even with Him. This is a fight that you will lose. Often when God punishes us, we think we can fight back. This is a lie. We must learn to take our punishment as a good child and trust in the hand of the Father.

CHALLENGE

Today, if the LORD is disciplining you, receive it as a child for it is by the hand of the Father.

Pray with me: LORD you are good, and you are God. God, thank you for fighting for me. LORD forgive me for the times I have tried to fight against your hand working in my life, even when it brought destruction. Thank you. AMEN

YOUR REFLECTIONS:

5 For you took my silver and gold
and carried my finest treasures to
your temples.

6 You sold the people of Judah and
Jerusalem to the Greeks to remove
them far from their own territory.

7 Look, I am about to rouse them up
from the place where you sold them;
I will bring retribution on your
heads.

8 I will sell your sons and daughters
to the people of Judah, and they will
sell them to the Sabeans, to a distant
nation, for the Lord has spoken.

9 Proclaim this among the nations:

Prepare for holy war;

rouse the warriors;

let all the men of war advance and
attack!

10 Beat your plows into swords

and your pruning knives into spears.

Let even the weakling say, "I am a
warrior."

11 Come quickly, all you
surrounding nations;

gather yourselves.

Bring down your warriors there,
Lord.

VERSE 5-6

5 For you took my silver and gold and carried my finest
treasures to your temples.
6 You sold the people of Judah and Jerusalem to the
Greeks to remove them far from their own territory.

Here, we see the crimes of Tyre and Sidon. They took what belonged to the LORD and placed them in their temples. They sold the people of Judah and Jerusalem to the Greeks. The sin is they took what was holy to the LORD and gave it to what was not HOLY.

When we take what is holy to the LORD and give it to false idols, we sin against the LORD. The very gold that was in the presence of the LORD, Tyre and Sidon placed in idol worship.

CHALLENGE

Have you ever taken what was holy to the LORD and simply gave it to idols? Often the very thing that we give up is our time. Today reclaim your time to the LORD.

YOUR REFLECTIONS:

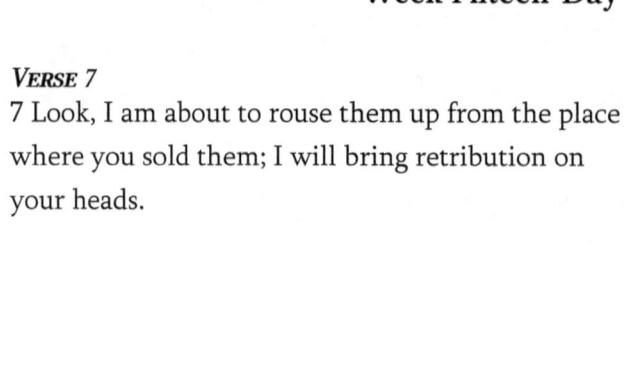

VERSE 7

7 Look, I am about to rouse them up from the place
where you sold them; I will bring retribution on
your heads.

God tells Tyre and Sidon that the very people that have been taken from Him, He will raise up to bring punishment as vengeance for the wrong against His people. This rousing is the Spirit of God that he will blow upon and pour out onto His people.

Vengeance is mine says the LORD. The LORD knows and is ever aware of what is going on in our lives. The people in Greece may have thought that God forgot about them, but God is ever there, and He is mighty to save.

CHALLENGE

Today, remember that God loves you and does not forget about you. You are on His mind and He can save you.

YOUR REFLECTIONS:

VERSE 8

8 I will sell your sons and daughters to the people of
Judah, and they will sell them to the Sabeans, to a distant
nation, for the Lord has spoken.

The same people who killed Job's servants and livestock are the same people God
says he will sell the offspring of Tyre and Sidon to. This is a very fearful sight for
the people of Tyre. They were not merciful to the people of God. Mercy is not
getting what you deserve. This is forgiveness.

Where mercy is shown, it is also given. Had Tyre and Sidon been merciful to the
people of Judah and Jerusalem, God would have been merciful to them. We are to
be encouraged and reminded that God shows mercy to the merciful.

CHALLENGE

Have you seen God's mercy in your life? Have you been merciful to your
neighbor? Today strive to be merciful to those who hurt you.

YOUR REFLECTIONS:

VERSE 9

9 Proclaim this among the nations:

Prepare for holy war;

rouse the warriors;

let all the men of war advance and attack!

Prepare for war. Time of war means there is no peace in the land. This is a battle that will involve the nations of the world, for it is the day of the LORD. The men of war are ever ready for the command of their commander.

When there is war, we can only pray for peace. When it is the day of the LORD, we can only run to the Father. Some are not cut out for war and some are not cut out for battle. Those who cannot fight run to the tower of refuge who is the LORD.

CHALLENGE

Today in the war of life and destruction, run to the LORD for His name is a strong tower.

YOUR REFLECTIONS:

VERSE 10

10 Beat your plows into swords

and your pruning knives into spears.

Let even the weakling say, "I am a warrior."

In the day of the LORD, there will be a transition from a time of peace to a time of war. Tools that were used for farming have now become tools of war. Those who are not equipped for the battle rush to the front lines. This is a transition of hope and rebuilding.

This transition is for the people to understand that this hope and rebuilding will last longer than a season. To destroy your equipment for war is to imply that war will be long, and there will not be time to plant and reap the harvest. The restoration takes time and must come to fulfillment.

CHALLENGE

Today, pray for patience in the LORD. Trust in Him through the process of the war of life.

YOUR REflECTIONS:

VERSE 11

11 Come quickly, all you surrounding nations;

gather yourselves.

Bring down your warriors there, Lord.

Come quickly, LORD. Judge the people on earth for the sin of their hearts. Let not one person be left out in your righteous judgment. A call for God to bring down His warriors on the people.

God is doing a work that we may not understand. He is leaving everything for His own time. Your destruction has a blessing attached to it. We must remain faithful to the one who is faithful when we are faithless.

CHALLENGE

Today, pray in the comfort of who God is.

Pray with me: LORD, you are good, and you are God. Come, Lord Jesus, Come. AMEN

YOUR REFLECTIONS:

12 Let the nations be roused

and come to the Valley of Jehoshaphat,

for there I will sit down

to judge all the surrounding nations.

13 Swing the sickle

because the harvest is ripe.

Come and trample the grapes

because the winepress is full;

the wine vats overflow

because the wickedness of the nations is extreme.

14 Multitudes, multitudes

in the valley of decision!

For the day of the Lord is near

in the valley of decision.

15 The sun and moon will grow dark,

and the stars will cease their shining.

16 The Lord will roar from Zion

and make his voice heard from Jerusalem;

heaven and earth will shake.

But the Lord will be a refuge for his people,

a stronghold for the Israelites.

VERSE 12

12 Let the nations be roused

and come to the Valley of Jehoshaphat,

for there I will sit down

to judge all the surrounding nations.

The time of judgment for the nations is at hand. The LORD will sit on His throne and judge the world. Everyone will be held accountable for their sin. This is the judgment of the heart of man. This is God seeing who is with Him and who has rejected Him and His Word.

The day of judgment for the LORD is only scary if you are not in Christ. If you are in Christ, then you have nothing to fear. As your turn comes and you stand before the throne, God will say well done, my good and faithful servant.

CHALLENGE

This is what we long to hear at the judgment seat of Christ. Will you hear those words? Has your heart been for the LORD in your time of destruction? Today, check your heart and see if it is really for the LORD.

YOUR REFLECTIONS:

VERSE 13

13 Swing the sickle

because the harvest is ripe.

Come and trample the grapes

because the winepress is full;

the wine vats overflow

because the wickedness of the nations is extreme.

The harvest is ripe and ready for reaping. God is swinging His sickle, separating the sheep from the goats. This trampling of the grapes to fill the vats is a representation of God's wrath. For God's wrath to be poured out on all mankind, it must reach a certain point. Once that point is reached, the wrath of God will be poured out on the whole world.

God's cup is steadily being filled and has continued to be filled throughout history. Where we stand in our destruction does not determine our end, this simply shows and encourages us to lean further into the love of God, for He will take care of those He loves.

CHALLENGE
The wrath of God will be poured out on all men. Today, trust God and pray for those who do not know the Son, that their eyes may be open.

YOUR REFLECTIONS:

VERSE 14
14 Multitudes, multitudes

in the valley of decision!

For the day of the Lord is near

in the valley of decision.

The valley of decision represents the hearts of the people toward the LORD. This valley is vast, and it is full of different deterrents that are designed to pull the children of God away from His love. This is a decision of the heart. Will the people choose God and be saved, or will they choose their sin and perish?

The heart is deceitful, who can trust it. We must check our hearts daily to see if we are fully committed to the LORD. This lifetime process is only conquered by the day-to-day devotion to the LORD.

CHALLENGE
Today, is your heart fully for the LORD, or is something pulling it away from the LOVE of the Father? Today, check your heart.

YOUR REFLECTIONS:

VERSE 15
15 The sun and moon will grow dark,

and the stars will cease their shining.

The sun turning to darkness and the stars ceasing their shine is a sign of the end. In the end, we will not need the sun, for the glory and holiness of God will be our light. For the sun to stop shining in the day of judgment means that God is saying, choose me, for you have nothing else. The sun won't shine on you. You won't have any light apart from me. I am the light of Life. Come to me and see.

This is a huge attentiveness in the detail of the LORD. He constantly shows us that we cannot do this on our own. We cannot handle eternity in ourselves. We are either with Him or apart from him in eternal darkness.

CHALLENGE
Today, pray for those who are close to you that they may see the light of LIFE.

YOUR REFLECTIONS:

VERSE 16
16 The Lord will roar from Zion

and make his voice heard from Jerusalem;

heaven and earth will shake.

But the Lord will be a refuge for his people,

a stronghold for the Israelites.

God is roaring on Mount Zion, saying come to me! Choose me for I will heal and save you. His voice is heard throughout the earth, and no one can say they haven't heard it. He stands and cries out for your heart to come to Him.

Man will be without excuses in the presence of the LORD. He is now calling us through His WORD. To hear Him calling through His WORD, you must be in His WORD to hear Him calling for you.

CHALLENGE
Have you been in His word today? Have you heard him calling? What are His words saying about Him today?

YOUR REfleCTIONS:

VERSE 16
16 The Lord will roar from Zion

and make his voice heard from Jerusalem;

<u>heaven and earth will shake.</u>

<u>But the Lord will be a refuge for his people,</u>

<u>a stronghold for the Israelites.</u>

Such assurance that the LORD brings for His people. He calls and he not only calls, but he also provides safety for His people. The earth shakes at the sound of the LORD. This brings terror; however, he is also providing safety from the terror of destruction. He is their refuge.

God is the security from the destruction of the world. He is ever calling. The world shakes at the sound of His voice, only to imply the severity of His command to run to Him. Come to Him NOW.

CHALLENGE
Today, if you haven't started running, RUN. If you haven't started crying out, CRY OUT NOW.

Pray with me: LORD, you are good, and you are God. LORD, thank you for calling me to your love. Thank you for pulling my heart towards your everlasting LOVE. God give me the boldness to share your love today. AMEN

YOUR REfLECTIONS:

17 Then you will know

that I am the Lord your God,

who dwells in Zion, my holy mountain.

Jerusalem will be holy,

and foreigners will never overrun it again.

18 In that day

the mountains will drip with sweet wine,

and the hills will flow with milk.

All the streams of Judah will flow with water,

and a spring will issue from the Lord's house,

watering the Valley of Acacias.

19 Egypt will become desolate,

and Edom a desert wasteland,

because of the violence done to the people of Judah

in whose land they shed innocent blood.

20 But Judah will be inhabited forever,

and Jerusalem from generation to generation.

21 I will pardon their bloodguilt,

which I have not pardoned,

for the Lord dwells in Zion.

VERSE 17
17 Then you will know

that I am the Lord your God,

who dwells in Zion, my holy mountain.

Jerusalem will be holy,

and foreigners will never overrun it again.

The people of God will know that He is the LORD because of His judgment and salvation. After He calls to His people to decide who to serve, He then provides safety in the time of trouble for His children.

God throughout scripture shows us He is the LORD in many ways. Sometimes it is through His wrath, and other times, it is through His wonders. Often, we look for the latter. We don't want to see God bringing destruction, we prefer to see him bringing peace and hope. What if one of the ways that God decides to bring peace and hope is through the destructions in our lives? Then we will truly know that He is the LORD.

CHALLENGE
And, you will know that I am the LORD. How do you know that God is LORD? Is it through destruction or peace?

YOUR REFLECTIONS:

VERSE 17

17 Then you will know

that I am the Lord your God,

who dwells in Zion, my holy mountain.

<u>Jerusalem will be holy,</u>

<u>and foreigners will never overrun it again.</u>

In the end, Jerusalem will be safe and set apart. It will no longer fear invasion from foreign powers. This is referring to the new Jerusalem in the kingdom of God. This is a prophetic word to encourage the people of God in their current suffering.

Oh, how the LORD encourages us to remain faithful in the destruction. In Him, having a new Jerusalem set for us, we witness that when he says all things for the good of those who love him, He means all things, and that includes the kingdom of God.

CHALLENGE

The storm is now over. Have you seen the good? Are you looking forward to the good that God provides?

YOUR REFLECTIONS:

VERSE 18

18 In that day

the mountains will drip with sweet wine,

and the hills will flow with milk.

All the streams of Judah will flow with water,

and a spring will issue from the Lord's house,

watering the Valley of Acacias.

God will provide for His people. In the kingdom, after the day of the LORD, God has prepared the promised land for His people. His spirit will be throughout His holy mountain, and there will not be an empty heart that the spirit has not touched. The living water will flow from the throne of God, and all who drink it will taste and see that the LORD is good. They will be satisfied with their God and no longer seek pleasure from created things.

This is full restoration; this is the fullness of God completed for His people. This is what we as children look forward to.

CHALLENGE

Today, pray and thank God that He has a place ready and prepared for you to be with Him for all eternity.

YOUR REFLECTIONS:

VERSE 19

19 Egypt will become desolate,

and Edom a desert wasteland,

because of the violence done to the people of Judah

in whose land they shed innocent blood.

God has not finished dealing with the people that have sinned against Him by invading His land and attacking His people. Egypt for the role they played in attacking and enslaving the people of God; Edom for turning their brothers into their attackers and hunting down those who were trying to escape their invaders. God will soon destroy them, and they will pay for their sin against the LORD.

In the unrepentant heart, the LORD does not forget. The heart that is turned away from the LORD will be judged on the day of the LORD. We are called to run and repent in all things that are contrary to scripture and biblical living.

CHALLENGE

Today, check your heart and pray for repentance as the LORD washes you with the blood of His Son, so that you may have fellowship with Him.

YOUR REflECTIONS:

VERSE 20

20 But Judah will be inhabited forever,

and Jerusalem from generation to generation.

Where other nations will be destroyed forever, in God's kingdom, there will be life and life to the full. The new earth will be different, and the standard will be met. God will reign over the earth.

Jerusalem will last forever. The people of God will be in peace forever in the presence of the LORD. We are the children. Destruction will have no power to separate us from the LOVE OF THE FATHER.

CHALLENGE

Today, pray for those who do not see. And thank the LORD for His grace upon your life.

YOUR REFLECTIONS:

VERSE 21

21 I will pardon their bloodguilt,

which I have not pardoned,

for the Lord dwells in Zion.

God will avenge us in all things. He has already avenged us from Sin. He has already rescued us from our destruction. The LORD dwelling in Zion is a sign that He will not move or go anywhere where he cannot be found by His children. He dwells in Zion for our sake.

Life will bring destruction to our lives. Sometimes God is the one that brings and allows the destruction to happen to you and me. The army is under His command. In our repentant hearts, He heals, and He saves. He is ever standing and calling out for us. We simply need to put our ears to His Word and listen. Life will bring destruction, however, there is always a blessing in the destruction. We simply need to turn to God to find it.

CHALLENGE

Today, understand that destruction comes and goes in life, pray to God that you may see the blessing in the destruction.

Pray with me: LORD, you are good, and you are God. LORD, thank you for the destruction in my LIFE. I pray that I get to the place where I run to you with everything. LORD, let me tear my heart, not just my clothes in repentance. I love you, God. Thank you for allowing me to see the blessing in the lesson of destruction.

YOUR Reflections:

www.ingramcontent.com/pod-product-compliance
Lightning Source LLC
Chambersburg PA
CBHW070724130626
46553CB00005B/2131